sport snaps
paul harris

19 Steve Yzerman
the quiet captain

This book is dedicated to Charlie L. Harris and the late Ellen R. Harris. They didn't start out with a lot of material wealth, but they gave their children gifts that are far more valuable.

P.H.

PHOTO CREDITS:

Allsport
1 [R. Stewart], 4 [R. Stewart], 8 [R. Laberge],
10 [J. Jacobsohn], 19, 22, 25 [R. Stewart],
36 [G. Cratty], 47 [R. Laberge], 49 [D. Pensinger],
53 [R. Laberge], 55 Left [S. Dunn], 56 [T. Pidgeon].

BBS
Front Cover [B. Bennett], 3 [S. Levy],
5 [B. Bennett], 7 [B. Bennett], 11 [B. Bennett],
12 [B. Bennett], 14 [B. Bennett], 16 [B. Bennett],
18 [B. Bennett], 20 [B. Bennett], 26 [B. Bennett],
28 [B. Bennett], 29 [B. Bennett], 30 [J. Hayt],
34 [S. Levy], 37 [B. Bennett], 38 [M. Hicks],
40 [B. Bennett], 41 [S. Levy], 42 [A. Foxall],
44 [B. Bennett], 46 [J. McIsaac], 50 [B. Bennett],
51 [M. Buckner], 52 [B. Bennett], 54 [B. Bennett],
55 Right [B. Bennett].

Detroit Free Press
6 [M. Schroeder].

Paul Harris' photo courtesy of *Hockey Weekly*.

© 2000 GHB Publishers, L.L.C.
All rights reserved.

No part of this book may be reproduced or transmitted in any form or by any means, electronic or mechanical, including photocopying and recording, or by any information storage retrieval system, without permission in writing from GHB Publishers, except for inclusion of brief quotations in an acknowledged review.

Printed by Pinnacle Press, Inc.
in the United States of America.

Edited by Tami Lent.

Designed by Werremeyer Creative.

**LIBRARY OF CONGRESS
CATALOG CARD NUMBER 99-68786**

table of contents

The Event Steve Yzerman Will Never Forget	page 4
Steve Yzerman Profile	page 6
chapter one: The Early Years	page 9
chapter two: A Rising Star	page 17
chapter three: Empty Numbers	page 27
chapter four: A New Era	page 35
chapter five: Finally…The Cup	page 43
Bowman Comments	page 54
Game-Day Routine	page 56

the event 19
STEVE YZERMAN WILL NEVER FORGET

When the Red Wings defeated the Philadelphia Flyers in Game 4 of the 1997 Stanley Cup Finals to win the Stanley Cup, Detroit's victory allowed Steve Yzerman to finally stand on the ice and hold hockey's most sacred piece of hardware above his head. It also completed a 14-season journey, filled with triumph and heartbreak. The Red Wings had finally achieved the title of the NHL's best of the best. It was a dream come true for Yzerman, the Red Wings and Red Wings fans.

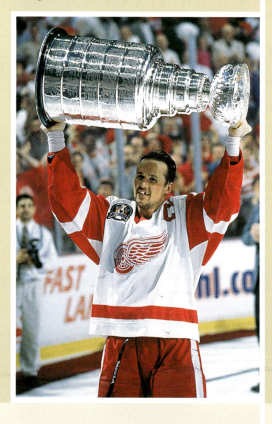

the quiet captain

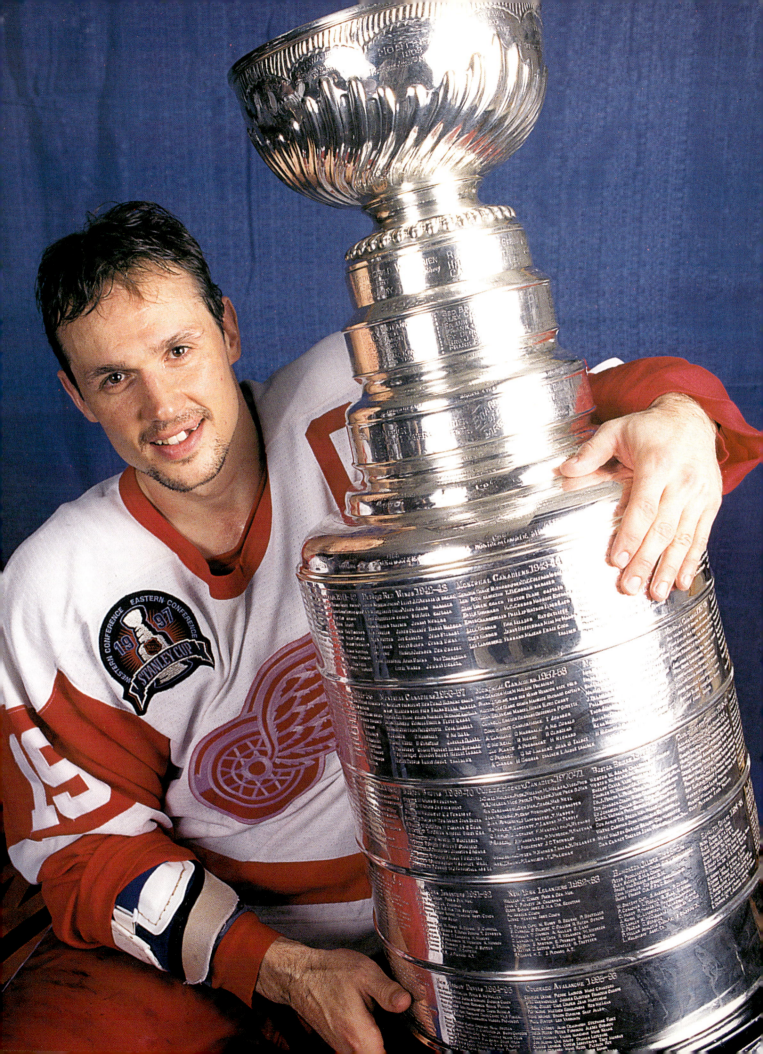

STEVE YZERMAN

profile 19

BORN:
MAY 9, 1965,
CRANBROOK, BRITISH COLUMBIA

FAMILY:
WIFE, LISA;
DAUGHTERS, ISABELLA, MARIA
AND SOPHIA

PERSON THAT MOST INFLUENCED HIM: His father, Ron. He is a no-nonsense, hardworking man who was employed by the Canadian government. Steve clearly shows the influences of his father in his serious approach to life and hockey.

OFF-SEASON RECREATION: Steve spends portions of his summer at a lake cabin near Toronto.

WHAT HE MIGHT HAVE DONE HAD HE NOT PLAYED HOCKEY: With both his parents working in the Canadian government, it seems a lock that Yzerman would've continued his education had he not gone into the NHL at age 18. It's not difficult to imagine Yzerman in politics – he's smart, calculating and works hard at whatever he does.

HOW TO SURVIVE ON THE ROAD: Since the Red Wings are one of the most tightly knit teams in the NHL, Steve and some of his teammates typically go out to dinner and the movies together.

FAVORITE OFF-SEASON GETAWAY FROM HOCKEY: Spending time with his family at his suburban Detroit home. Steve is also an avid sports fan and watches football, baseball, golf and basketball on television. He's a long-time subscriber to *Sports Illustrated*.

FAVORITE NHL PLAYERS WHILE GROWING UP: Yzerman had two hockey heroes: Alex Delvecchio, Red Wings Hall of Fame center, and Bryan Trottier, New York Islanders and Pittsburgh Penguins Hall of Fame center. Yzerman was an admirer of Trottier from the time Trottier joined the NHL. Trottier's number was 19; Yzerman's number is 19. Interestingly enough, Yzerman has passed both of his childhood heroes on the all-time points and goals list.

BLOOD RAN DOWN THE SIDE OF STEVE YZERMAN'S FACE; THE DETROIT RED WINGS CAPTAIN WAS OBVIOUSLY ANGRY. IN THE OPENING MINUTES OF THE FIRST GAME OF THE FIRST ROUND OF THE 1999 STANLEY CUP PLAYOFFS, YZERMAN HAD TAKEN AN ELBOW FROM ANAHEIM CENTER STEVE RUCCHIN. NOT ONLY WAS YZERMAN UNHAPPY ABOUT THE NASTY CUT OVER ONE OF HIS EYES, BUT THERE WAS NO PENALTY CALLED ON THE PLAY. THIS MADE YZERMAN, ONE OF THE MOST RELENTLESS ATHLETES ANYBODY WOULD EVER WANT TO MEET, EVEN MORE DETERMINED.

RED WINGS RECORD | most points by a rookie: 87

chapter one: The Early Years

A few minutes later, Yzerman was positioned just to the left of Anaheim goaltender Guy Hebert. A shot from the blue line went wide of the net and bounced off the backboards directly to Yzerman, who, without stopping the puck, drilled it into a miniscule opening on Hebert's short side from a seemingly impossible angle. The goal tied the game at 1-1, and Yzerman reacted as if he were getting revenge from the earlier elbow. But he wasn't done yet. Just 31 seconds into the second period, Hebert made the save on a shot, but Yzerman – this time on Hebert's right – snapped a shot into the upper corner of the net.

The Ducks, however, were pesky on this night. The Red Wings led 4-3 with less than 90 seconds left in regulation time. The puck was cleared into Anaheim's zone, and the Ducks' Teemu Selanne raced after it with Detroit's Brendan Shanahan right on his tail. Selanne got to the puck, but Shanahan got just enough of Selanne's body to knock it loose. At the same time, rookie goaltender Tom Askey (who had replaced Hebert because of an injury) tried to race from

the crease and retrieve the puck. But Yzerman beat him to it, took a couple of strides and fired the puck into the empty net to clinch a 5-3 victory, completing the fourth hat trick of his Stanley Cup playoff career – a Red Wings team record.

The message was clear: Don't make Steve Yzerman mad.

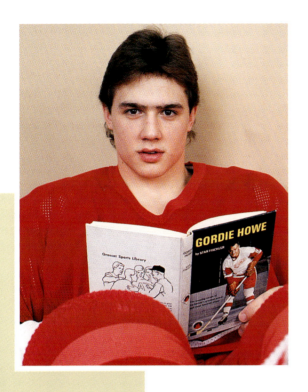

That kind of determination and talent has allowed Yzerman to become ninth on the NHL's all-time scoring list with 1483 points over a 16-season NHL career. His 592 goals are eleventh all-time, and his 891 assists tie him for tenth. He's the longest-serving captain in NHL history (he was named the Red Wings captain just before the 1986-87 season) and has led his team to back-to-back Stanley Cup titles in 1997 and 1998 after years of disappointing playoff eliminations. While these statistics are certainly impressive, they really tell just a small part of the story of Steve Yzerman – a story of perseverance and determination that has won him the respect and admiration of his coaches, peers and teammates since he first started playing hockey as a youngster in a small town in Canada.

Steve's parents, Ron and Jean Yzerman, began raising their family in Cranbrook, British Columbia, located about 45 miles west of the province of Alberta. Ron was a government official and, in the mid-'70s, was transferred to Ottawa. The Yzermans and their five children – Roni Jean; Michael, who went on to play college hockey; Steve; Gary; and Chris – settled in the suburb of Nepean. Raising five children is certainly a daunting task, but there was always order in the Yzerman household.

chapter one: The Early Years

"Ron was a government worker who ran a tight ship," said former NHL goaltender and current ESPN analyst Darren Pang. "When things got out of line, he was pretty quick to get on top of it. Ron is the kind of guy that when you're younger and you do something wrong, he gets your attention. Ron liked to keep everyone in line, and Steve reflected that [trait]." As he became one of the best young players in the area, Yzerman continued to mirror the values of his parents. "They just went about their business and worked hard," said Pang of Ron and Jean. "The kids admired that."

Pang, who is one of Yzerman's best friends, first met the future Red Wings star when Steve was 14. Beginning in the 1980-81 season, they were teammates with the Junior A Tier II Nepean Raiders. "He was unbelievable," said Pang of Yzerman, who as a 15-year-old was playing against and dominating 16- and 17-year-olds. "...He never quit. Besides the fact he was a highly skilled player, the thing that stood out in my mind was that he never quit. As the goalie on his team who stood and watched him, I thought he was fantastic. When we needed a goal, he got the puck and he didn't give it up until either he scored or he passed it to somebody else who scored."

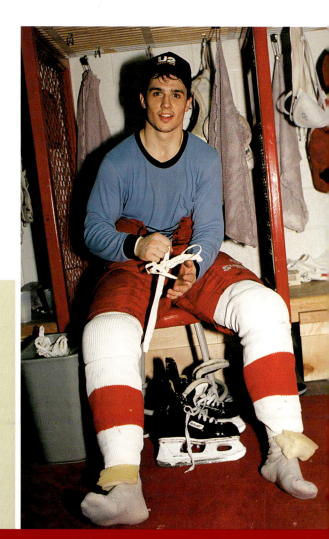

The following season, Yzerman moved on to Major Junior Hockey when he was drafted by the Peterborough Petes of the Ontario Hockey League. He then hired his first agent, Gus Badali. The young man that Badali got to know was unquestionably Ron and Jean's son. "His personality was quiet, a little bit shy. Except for when he got on the ice," said Badali. "He was determined to get the job done. And when he got it done, he wasn't looking for any pats on the back. I know he was a real gentleman at that age. He was just quiet. I'm sure he let his hair down with guys his own age." Pang confirmed that suspicion. "The perception of Steve is that he doesn't really open up. He thinks about what he says, and that's different these days," said Pang. "But when he's around a group of people that he knows really well, he's in on most of the jokes and is actually a pretty funny guy."

> **"I always thought he was kind of a quiet leader.**
> And when I played with him, nothing changed [that perception]."
>
> DINO CICCARELLI, FORMER RED WINGS TEAMMATE

In his two seasons with Peterborough, Yzerman put up good numbers but not the spectacular statistics that players of his ability usually put up in Major Junior Hockey. The reason was the coaching philosophy of then-Peterborough coach Dick Todd, who later went on to be an assistant coach in the NHL with the New York Rangers. Todd believed in using four lines on a consistent basis. Even when the Petes had a power play, the next line would take their shift. That goes against the usual hockey practice, particularly at the junior level, of using the better players on special teams. Todd's system also meant that NHL scouts would not have the chance to see Yzerman on the ice as much as they would other forwards eligible for the 1983 NHL Entry Draft. While Yzerman would've liked to have played more, he made the best of the situation.

RED WINGS RECORD | most goals by a rookie: 39

chapter one: The Early Years

Red Wings general manager Jim Devellano and the Red Wings scouts were certainly able to see Yzerman's ability when they watched the youngster play. "When we saw them [the Petes] play, there was very little doubt that he was a highly intelligent and skilled player on his shifts," said Devellano. Yzerman – along with Brian Lawton, Sylvain Turgeon and Pat LaFontaine – was considered to be among the cream of the crop, but no one was sure in what order these four players would go.

Less than a year before the draft, the Norris family, who had owned the Red Wings since 1932, had sold the team to Little Caesars Pizza owners Mike and Marian Ilitch. The 1983 draft was to be the first of the Ilitch era and it was entrusted to Devellano, who had helped lead the New York Islanders to four-straight Stanley Cups from 1980-83. In addition to the pressure of making the new ownership's first pick (fourth overall), Devellano also had another problem.

NHL | **fourth player selected in 1983 NHL Entry Draft**

Red Wings fans would've liked nothing more than for the Red Wings to select the hometown boy, Pat LaFontaine. Although LaFontaine was playing junior hockey in Quebec, he had grown up in the Detroit suburb of Waterford and had played in the Detroit area. Devellano says it's likely that he would have taken LaFontaine if he had been available. A hometown hero would've been the perfect medicine for Detroit's attendance ills. But, as it turned out, Devellano didn't have that chance.

> "It certainly makes me very proud that the guy we took first to try and construct the franchise has really worked out well. It's nice that he's been able **to play his whole career in one city and win the fans' hearts.** I don't know how much more you're going to see that in sports."
>
> JIM DEVELLANO, RED WINGS SENIOR VICE PRESIDENT AND FORMER GM

The Minnesota North Stars took Lawton with the first pick, and the Hartford Whalers selected Turgeon second. Devellano's old team, the Islanders, chose LaFontaine, leaving 18-year-old Yzerman for the Red Wings. "LaFontaine went on to have a good career. But over the years, Yzerman has proved to be the better pick," said Devellano. Devellano also said that Todd's four-line system may have allowed Yzerman to be available to Detroit at the fourth pick. "He [Yzerman] probably would've went one, two or three if the coach would've played his best players more," said Devellano.

THE FIRST TIME GOALTENDER GREG STEFAN SAW YZERMAN, HE DIDN'T EVEN THINK YZERMAN WAS A HOCKEY PLAYER. "I SAW THIS YOUNG KID COMING IN [THE HOTEL] AND I THOUGHT HE WAS LOOKING FOR AN AUTOGRAPH," SAID STEFAN, WHO WOULD SPEND SEVEN SEASONS AS YZERMAN'S TEAMMATE. "MY FIRST RECOLLECTION OF HIM IS [AS] A BABY FACE, AND HE WAS SO QUIET. HE NEVER SAID BOO." BUT HIS TALENTS SPOKE VOLUMES, AND HE EASILY MADE THE TEAM OUT OF TRAINING CAMP IN 1983. HE ALSO QUICKLY MADE A REPUTATION AROUND THE LEAGUE AS AN OUTSTANDING YOUNG PLAYER.

1483

NHL | **career points: 1483**

chapter two: A Rising Star

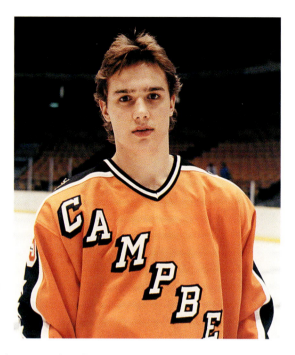

"We had heard a lot about this guy, this 'Yisserman' guy," said current Red Wings associate coach Dave Lewis, who was a defenseman with the New Jersey Devils when Yzerman was a rookie. "Each year the veteran players always watched out for guys who might take their jobs or of just young players who were making a name for themselves, and those names would make the rounds." When the Devils finally played the Red Wings, Lewis saw that young No. 19 had quite a bit of ability. "As it turns out, in the open ice, he was very good," said Lewis. But at only 18 and playing against mature men, Yzerman did have one big disadvantage: He was only about 5 feet 10 inches tall and 180 pounds. "I remember going into the corners with him," said Lewis. "He didn't have enough strength to protect the puck. In the open ice, he was okay. But in the corners, he just didn't have the strength." Despite that, Yzerman finished the season with 39 goals and 48 assists for 87 points, setting the records for goals and points by a Red Wings rookie. Although he finished second to Buffalo's Tom Barrasso in the race for the Calder Trophy, which is awarded to the National Hockey League's top rookie, he was named *The Sporting News* Rookie of the Year. That season, Detroit made the playoffs for the first time since the 1977-78 season.

Prior to the 1984-85 season, Yzerman was picked to play for Team Canada in the 1984 Canada Cup Tournament. He played in four games as Canada won the tournament's gold medal by beating Sweden in the championship game. During the NHL season that followed, Yzerman continued to establish himself as one of the league's emerging stars. His goal production dropped to 30 but he had 59 assists for 89 points, two more than he had collected as a rookie. The Red Wings once again made the playoffs but were eliminated in the first round by the Chicago Blackhawks.

Despite the playoff losses, the first two years of Yzerman's NHL career not only showed his personal potential but were a ray of hope in the Red Wings franchise. The 1985-86 season began with great promise for Yzerman and the Red Wings, but things quickly unraveled. After 51 games, Yzerman had only 14 goals and 28 assists for 42 points. And, on January 31, 1986, he fractured his collarbone and missed the rest of the season. Yzerman was becoming an NHL star, but he was dealing with the first major injury of his young career. Furthermore, the Red Wings team was in shambles, finishing with the NHL's worst record.

> "Steve Yzerman is a quiet guy, but he always led by his play on the ice. **In the four years I coached him, he always came to play.**"
>
> JACQUES DEMERS, FORMER RED WINGS COACH

Looking for a spark, the Red Wings hired the charismatic Jacques Demers as their coach prior to the 1986-87 season. He was a coach who motivated his players with emotion and was always a favorite among media members because he loved to talk. It was obvious to Demers that Yzerman was his best player, and Demers wanted his best player to be his captain. So, during training camp in the fall of 1986, 21-year-old Yzerman was named the team's captain. He wasn't boisterous, but he worked hard and set an outstanding example. "Steve was never a talkative captain. He was a leader in work ethic and being prepared to play," said Stefan. "He never said much. At times he did, if there was something to be said. The guys respected him because of his hard work and honesty." Though he was young, Yzerman said being named captain ultimately helped his game. "If anything, it made me take games and practices more seriously," he said. "And it made me become a better hockey player." Yzerman did struggle a bit, particularly because he was such a young player on a team with a lot of veterans. "He had to learn the little skills of being the captain. Of dealing with teammates and coaches and ownership and the media," said Lewis.

chapter two: A Rising Star

The players who made up the Red Wings during the 1986-87 and 1987-88 seasons were a combination of youngsters establishing themselves in the NHL – Yzerman, Gerard Gallant, Petr Klima, Shawn Burr, Adam Oates, Bob Probert, Joe Kocur and Steve Chiasson – along with a group of hardworking veterans who had all of the savvy in the world, like Lewis, Harold Snepsts, Tim Higgins and goaltender Glen Hanlon. The Red Wings weren't the most talented team in the world, but they worked hard and played a physical style. Demers put Yzerman on the ice as much as possible in every situation. With Yzerman leading the way and Gallant and Probert riding shotgun, the Red Wings almost doubled their point production from the previous season. With 78 points, the Red Wings finished second in the Norris Division, qualifying for the Stanley Cup playoffs. Amazingly, the Cinderella Red Wings made it all the way to the Campbell Conference finals, where they lost to the Edmonton Oilers in five games. Yzerman was a big part of Detroit's playoff success, as he collected five goals and 13 assists for 18 points.

While he was still figuring out how to be a captain, Yzerman had just about figured out what it took to be an NHL star. "He felt he could play head-to-head with anybody," said Lewis. "I think, in his mind, he had to establish himself as a premier offensive player because that was what he was expected to do."

Hockey Tips for Young Players: IMPROVING YOUR SKATING

SKATE EVERY CHANCE YOU GET — WHETHER IT'S A GAME OR A PRACTICE, PLAYING PICKUP OR SHINNY WITH YOUR FRIENDS, OR EVEN JUST FREE SKATING WITHOUT STICKS AND PUCKS. IT'S IMPORTANT TO GET ON THE ICE AT EVERY OPPORTUNITY. SKATING IS THE MOST IMPORTANT SKILL THAT YOU HAVE AS A HOCKEY PLAYER. THE BETTER SKATER YOU ARE, THE BETTER PLAYER YOU'LL BE AND THE BETTER CHANCE YOU'LL HAVE TO ADVANCE TO HIGHER LEVELS.

> "He's far and away the **fastest healing athlete I've ever worked with.**"
>
> — JOHN WHARTON, RED WINGS TRAINER

And 1987-88 would be the season that Yzerman completed his ascension to NHL superstardom. Through 63 games, Yzerman had 49 goals and over 100 points. In the 64th game at Detroit's Joe Louis Arena on March 1, 1988, Yzerman got number 50 to become only the fourth Red Wing in history to reach that plateau. But on the history-making play, Yzerman also suffered a serious injury when his right leg went into one of the goal posts. He injured the ligaments of his right knee so seriously that the prevailing medical opinion was that his hockey career was in jeopardy. Yzerman was given a choice of either surgery or rehabilitation. He decided on rehabilitation and attacked it with everything that he had. "He had a career-ending type injury.... He never got that operated on," said Stefan. "There was talk that he would never be the same again. That he would lose a step. And you look at him, he hasn't lost too many yet. He was in the weight room twice a day working on every muscle surrounding that knee.... I've never seen anybody work that hard coming back from an injury."

RED WINGS RECORD | single-season most goals: 65 (1988-89)

chapter two: A Rising Star

While Yzerman was out with his injury, the Red Wings once again advanced to the Campbell Conference finals against the Oilers, who won the first two games in Edmonton. But when the series returned to Detroit, No. 19 was back in the Red Wings lineup. With their captain on the ice and the hometown crowd in a frenzy, the Red Wings got back into the series with a 5-2 victory over the Oilers. Once again, however, Yzerman and his teammates would be no match for the Oilers – who featured Wayne Gretzky, Mark Messier, Paul Coffey, Grant Fuhr and Jari Kurri. Edmonton won the next two games of the series and went on to win the Stanley Cup for the second-straight season and for the fourth time in five seasons. The Red Wings had gone farther than anyone expected them to go. Yzerman had joined the elite club of NHL 50-goal scorers – in only 64 games – and, for the first time, had shown the entire NHL his heart and determination. It wouldn't be the last time.

"He blocks shots, he battles with big defensemen.
You would like a guy like Steve Yzerman to be with you in a battle on the ice or a back alley."
DAVE LEWIS, RED WINGS ASSOCIATE COACH AND FORMER TEAMMATE

As the 1988-89 season approached, Yzerman had become a substantial presence in the National Hockey League and one of the most popular athletes in and around Detroit. Men gloried in his ability and his determination, youngsters idolized him and wanted to play like him and female fans swooned over his boyish good looks. There was also another reason for fans to love Yzerman; however, he made sure that they didn't find out about it. Shortly after he had become the team's captain, Yzerman began visiting sick children in Detroit-area hospitals. He didn't publicize it and he didn't want it publicized.

"Always on the side. Nobody ever knew," said Darren Pang of Yzerman's hospital visits. "It drove him crazy that there were guys who would visit hospitals and then publicize it." Dave Lewis believes more people should know about what Yzerman does for charities and children. "I don't think he's respected enough for his charitable work. Especially with Make-A-Wish," said Lewis. "He's very good with kids. I know of stories of him going to hospitals with no media and no publicity. That had nothing to do with it."

Hockey Tips for Young Players: OFF-ICE CONDITIONING

#2

WHILE THE GAME IS PLAYED ON THE ICE, A BIG PART OF THE PHYSICAL PREPARATION COMES OFF THE ICE IN THE FORM OF CONDITIONING. RUNNING, IN-LINE SKATING AND CYCLING ARE ALL GOOD WAYS TO REACH AND MAINTAIN A BASE OF AEROBIC OFF-ICE CONDITIONING. WHEN YOU REACH THE AGE OF 14, WEIGHTLIFTING MAY HELP YOU DEVELOP MORE AS A HOCKEY PLAYER. FOR A MORE DETAILED PROGRAM, YOU SHOULD CONSULT AN ACCREDITED PROFESSIONAL ATHLETIC TRAINER.

RED WINGS RECORD | single-season most assists: 90 (1988-89)

chapter two: A Rising Star

The success of Yzerman and his teammates under Demers in the previous two seasons had made it cool and fashionable to be a Red Wings fan again. The 1988-89 season began with the optimism of repeating or surpassing the success of the previous two seasons. During the off-season, the Red Wings acquired Paul MacLean from Winnipeg, and he immediately found a home on the right side with Yzerman and Gerard Gallant. That trio, with the biggest contribution from Yzerman, would become the highest scoring line in a single season in Red Wings history. Yzerman, Gallant and MacLean would combine for 319 points during the season, with 155 of them coming from Yzerman. The Red Wings finished first in the Norris Division that year, but they were eliminated in six games by the Chicago Blackhawks, a team that finished 14 points behind them in the regular season. Although he had five goals and five assists in the series, it would be the first of many times Yzerman, as captain, would have to explain a disappointing playoff elimination to the Detroit media.

Despite an early exit in the postseason, Yzerman's individual accomplishments had won the respect and admiration of his peers. That season, he won the Lester B. Pearson Award, which is voted on by the members of the NHL Players' Association. The players whom Yzerman skated against game after game chose him as the NHL's "most outstanding player." "That trophy meant so much [to Yzerman] because the players voted it to him over the Hart Trophy winner, who was Gretzky," said Pang. "He [Yzerman] was never a sour grapes guy. Never, 'I had a good year and I got robbed.'"

RED WINGS RECORD | most career short-handed goals: 45

Yzerman topped 100 points every year in the six seasons from 1987-88 until 1992-93 and averaged 55 goals, 67 assists and 122 points. It was one of the most dominant statistical runs by any player in NHL history. Still he remained in the shadows. There were two reasons for that: Wayne Gretzky and Mario Lemieux. Yzerman, a center, had the misfortune of having the best years of his career while the two greatest centers to ever play in the NHL were putting up unimaginable numbers. Though he was supremely talented, Yzerman's talent didn't match that of Gretzky or Lemieux, and Yzerman's teammates talents didn't match the talents of Gretzky's and Lemieux's teammates. He had to be content to be the NHL's "best mortal hockey player." But that didn't bother him. "That stuff [statistics] I could care less about. It means very little in your career," said Yzerman.

What did bother him was not being picked for the 1991 Canada Cup team. Coach Mike Keenan thought of Yzerman as a one-dimensional player who only cared about offense and didn't work on the defensive end. "I think the one thing that bothered him was that he didn't get picked for Team Canada one year," Lewis said. "He would've been effective playing a role and he would've been willing to do it. But Mike Keenan was the coach and didn't pick him. He was never one to talk much about his statistics versus somebody else's. But he would've liked to represent his country."

probably more talented than the two teams which had lost to Edmonton in the Campbell Conference finals, the players were beginning to tune Demers out. Demers was a great motivator who used emotion to get his players excited and ready to play, but that emotion is hard to sustain for more than a couple of years. The Red Wings' lack of stability severely tested Yzerman as the team's captain. Though he had learned much in his four seasons of wearing the "C," Detroit's situation in 1988-89 and 1989-90 caused cliques to form in the Red Wings locker room. Yzerman wasn't prepared to deal with that. "When you're a young guy in that position, you do some things right and you do some things wrong," said former NHL goaltender Mike Liut. The team would miss the playoffs, finishing last in the Norris Division with 70 points. Yzerman, however, continued to be one of the league's biggest offensive threats. His 62 goals and 65 assists for 127 points allowed him to finish third in the NHL scoring race behind Wayne Gretzky and Mark Messier.

NHL | career goals scored: 592

chapter three: Empty Numbers

Demers was replaced the following season by Bryan Murray, who had coached the Washington Capitals. Murray was also hired to be Detroit's general manager.

Things would get brighter for Yzerman and the Red Wings in a relatively short amount of time due to a string of highly successful drafts. These drafts added such players as Nicklas Lidstrom, Vladimir Konstantinov and goaltender Chris Osgood, but only one, Sergei Fedorov, made an immediate impact. Just 20 when the season began, Fedorov was a devastating combination of speed, strength and skill. It became immediately clear that he would become the second-line center that the Red Wings had craved for years to take pressure off Yzerman.

Though the Red Wings finished more than 25 points behind Chicago, the Norris Division's champion, they finished with a 34-38-4 record, good enough to qualify for the 1990-91 playoffs. Their playoff opponents were the St. Louis

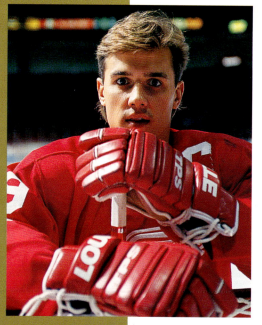

Blues, who were heavily favored because of their superior regular-season record. The series began in St. Louis, and Yzerman turned in a classic performance. He scored three goals to lead the Red Wings to a 6-3 victory. One of his goals came on a miraculous shot from the left face-off circle. Yzerman appeared to have only a small opening on Blues goaltender Vincent Riendeau's glove side, but he threaded the needle on the shot which beat Riendeau. Although Detroit went up three games to one, the Blues stormed back to win the last three games of the series. The Red Wings had made the playoffs in Murray's first season and, in Fedorov, they finally had another player who was in Yzerman's class in skill and offensive ability.

The captain would get more help in the 1991-92 season. Young players like Lidstrom and Konstantinov were now ready to play in the NHL, and off-season acquisitions, including Paul Ysebaert and Ray Sheppard, were transforming the Red Wings into one of the most talented teams in the league. The acquisitions of Ysebaert and Sheppard would become important off the ice for Yzerman as well, as all three would become good friends. In fact, Yzerman, Gerard Gallant, Steve Chiasson, Ysebaert and Sheppard became such good friends that teammates dubbed them "The Fab Five." Finally, Yzerman didn't have to score all the goals and get all of the points. Though his 1991-92 numbers "dropped" to 45 goals and 58 assists, the Red Wings' 320 goals were the fourth best overall in the NHL. More importantly, their 43-25-12 record gave them a conference-leading 98 points, which tied them for second in the entire NHL.

But as the season neared the playoffs, there was labor unrest between the NHL's owners and the National Hockey League Players' Association (NHLPA). In April, the NHLPA walked out for the NHL's first-ever league-wide players' strike, which threatened the Stanley Cup playoffs. Talks soon began. Yzerman, as the Red Wings player representative, sat on the players' side of the table; Mike Ilitch, as owner, sat on the owners' side. Although Ilitch had treated Red Wings players quite well, not every NHL owner was so generous. Yzerman wasn't there to face down Ilitch. He was there to make sure his fellow players got what he felt they deserved. The strike was settled in 10 days, and the playoffs began with great expectations for the Red Wings. After defeating Minnesota in the first round, Detroit's hopes were quickly dashed as they were swept by the Chicago Blackhawks. The team that had put up big numbers in the regular season fizzled in the playoffs, when checking is closer, goals are harder to come by and team defense is more important. It would not be the last time.

NHL | career games played: 1178

chapter three: Empty Numbers

But even more offensive talent was added before and during the 1992-93 season. On the day of the 1992 draft, the Red Wings acquired Dino Ciccarelli, one of the most prolific goal scorers in NHL history, from the Washington Capitals. He was so excited about the prospects of joining Yzerman and the rest of the Red Wings offensive juggernaut, he said, "We might never lose a game this season." And on January 29, 1993, the Red Wings acquired defenseman Paul Coffey, the highest-scoring defenseman in NHL history.

Surrounded by even more offensive talent, Yzerman had the second-most productive season of his NHL career. His 58 goals and 79 assists for 137 points placed him fourth in the league scoring race. Yzerman was also a plus-33, a career best. He led the Red Wings to an even better record than they had compiled the previous season, finishing only three points behind the Chicago Blackhawks in the Norris Division.

#3 Hockey Tips for Young Players: DEVELOPING AWARENESS

DON'T HAVE TUNNEL VISION ON THE ICE. ALWAYS KNOW WHAT'S GOING ON AROUND YOU, WHETHER YOU HAVE THE PUCK OR NOT. IF YOU HAVE THE PUCK, DON'T BECOME MESMERIZED BY IT. IF YOU'RE IN TRAFFIC, TRY TO DRAW A DEFENDER TO YOU AND THEN MAKE A PASS TO A TEAMMATE. IF YOU DON'T HAVE THE PUCK AND ARE ANTICIPATING A PASS, LOOK AROUND THE ICE AND SEE WHERE THE REST OF THE PLAYERS ARE. YOU HAVE TO KNOW WHAT YOU CAN DO WITH THE PUCK BEFORE YOU GET IT.

Once again, the Red Wings had proven they were among the NHL's best and most exciting teams during the regular season. But would they be able to pass the playoff test? Their first-round opponents were the Toronto Maple Leafs, a team that was the polar opposite of Detroit as far as style and play were concerned. While the Red Wings had been built for the regular season, the Maple Leafs were built for the playoffs. Once again, defense triumphed over offense – and the Red Wings – in seven games. The playoff loss cost Murray his job, and eventually Scotty Bowman accepted the Red Wings coaching position. Yzerman now had a coach – who had won six Stanley Cups and was already in the Hockey Hall of Fame – on his side. Or did he?

While Yzerman had enjoyed unqualified personal success in his first 10 seasons in the National Hockey League, the team disappointments the Red Wings had suffered were taking a toll on him. Ron and Jean had brought up their son in an environment where you were expected to work hard, succeed and not be too pleased with yourself afterwards. So what happened when you worked hard and didn't succeed? Sure, Yzerman was having personal success. But his team hadn't won the Stanley Cup, so he hadn't achieved his ultimate goal. The result was that Yzerman wasn't always the happiest individual in the Red Wings dressing room. "He's a very serious person. There have been times when he got to the rink, and he didn't look around and smell the coffee," said Pang about Yzerman. "I didn't believe that he went to the rink really happy every day. Going through what he did with the Red Wings in the 80s, the close calls and then the disappointments of the 90s had taken their toll on him."

NHL | career assists: 891

chapter three: Empty Numbers

People were also beginning to question Yzerman's abilities as a leader. "Could he ever win?" fans and the media asked. Sure, he could pile up statistics from here to the moon. But winning was what it was all about. And, so far, he hadn't done it. There was no question Yzerman knew how to produce offense. But because he had always been under such pressure to do so in his first few seasons in the NHL, he didn't know about the subtleties – like winning face-offs and backchecking – that meant the difference between winning and losing in the playoffs. And despite having worn the "C" for the previous seven seasons, Yzerman still struggled with the duties of a captain. It was likely that his own unhappiness was a part of it. When he did speak, his teammates listened to him. He didn't, however, speak to most of the members of the Red Wings often. There were times when he only communicated with Gallant, Chiasson, Sheppard and Ysebaert.

Not surprisingly, the Detroit Red Wings were a team of cliques when Bowman arrived on the scene during the summer of 1993. One of his first moves was to subtract Paul Ysebaert, one of "The Fab Five." With Bowman on board, even bigger things were expected of the Red Wings in 1993-94. Unfortunately, on October 21, in a 6-2 victory over the Winnipeg Jets, Yzerman suffered a herniated disc when he was hit from behind into the boards. Yzerman would miss 26 games that season with the injury.

But even with their captain out, the Red Wings didn't miss a beat. That's because Fedorov stepped into the role of the team's number one center and even wore the "C" in Yzerman's absence. When Yzerman returned to the lineup, he continued to produce but became more of a playmaker. He finished with 24 goals and 58 assists in 58 games. Also when he returned, he faced something that he hadn't had to deal with since he broke into the league: criticism from the coach. While on the surface Bowman didn't do much to change the team's run-and-gun style, he made it a point of regularly dressing down Yzerman about his defensive shortcomings and lack of detail in full earshot of his teammates. Yzerman was stunned and hurt; however, because of his upbringing and personality, he didn't make a public issue out of it.

On the ice, the Red Wings were once again an offensive juggernaut. Their 356 goals were the most in the NHL, but, despite Bowman's presence, the team still gave up a lot of goals. The Red Wings and their fans went into the 1993-94 playoffs with all of the confidence in the world. But it would turn out to be a fool's confidence. Not only did the Red Wings lose in the first round again, but this time they lost to an eighth-seeded team, the San Jose Sharks, which had only existed for three years. Of all the playoff disappointments of the past few seasons, this one was the worse. The repercussions of the loss would reverberate throughout the Red Wings organization and set the stage for a dominant four-season run.

Before the 1994-95 season began, Bowman, who held Yzerman and Coffey responsible for the team's defensive shortcomings, met with both players. The coach told them that it was important that they both bought into the new defensive system, the "left-wing lock." Bowman felt that if the rest of the team saw the two future Hall of Famers, who had always piled up points, embrace this new style, everyone would follow.

NHL | **All-Star appearances: 9**

chapter four: A New Era

Now, armed with the left-wing lock, the Red Wings and Yzerman couldn't wait to get the season started. But the NHL's team owners could. They decided something had to be done about the spiraling player salaries and bad financial predicaments in which many of the teams found themselves. After the exhibition season, the owners locked out the players. In all, the lockout lasted 103 days. Finally, an agreement was reached and the NHL season – in which each team would play 48 games – began on January 20, 1995.

The left-wing lock and the additions of forward Doug Brown, left winger Bob Errey and defenseman Viacheslav Fetisov produced immediate dividends as Detroit won the 1995 Presidents' Trophy, which went to the team with the NHL's best regular-season record. Keeping the goals-against down had become the team's objective, and the Red Wings had the second lowest total in the league with 117; however, the Red Wings still scored plenty of goals.

While Yzerman did buy into the Red Wings' new defensive system and was immediately effective at carrying out his defensive responsibilities, his production suffered. He scored only 12 goals and 26 assists in the shortened season, suffering through a career-high 15-game goalless streak and less than 15 games later began a six-game pointless streak.

Despite the team's outstanding regular season, Red Wings fans were understandably nervous about the postseason. But the Wings methodically dispatched the Dallas Stars in five games, San Jose in four games and Chicago in five games to reach the Stanley Cup finals for the first time since 1966. It would be Yzerman's first trip to the finals and his first opportunity to win the cherished Stanley Cup. Before the finals against the New Jersey Devils began, Yzerman talked about the Stanley Cup. "I don't remember if I've really actually touched it or gotten close to it. The last few years, I've made it a point of not really going near it," he said. "I really have no desire to get near it until I get the opportunity to win it."

The Red Wings were heavily favored among most observers. Their dominant regular season had continued during the playoffs as they won 12 of 14 games during the first three rounds. They also had marquee names like Yzerman, Coffey, Fedorov and Ciccarelli. The Devils were perceived as a bunch of no-name players who played a boring style. Nevertheless, the Devils outclassed the Red Wings and won the Stanley Cup in four games. While Yzerman played well, it was clear he wasn't himself. A knee injury that he suffered earlier in the playoffs wasn't completely healed, but he was giving it everything he had. He simply wasn't a factor, and a late goal in Game 3 would be his only point in the series.

NHL | one hundred point seasons: 6

chapter four: A New Era

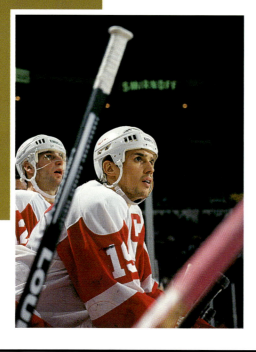

As the Red Wings opened training camp for the 1995-96 season, the word was out that Bowman felt he had to make a drastic change on the team. Fedorov and Keith Primeau appeared to be an outstanding 1-2 center combination for years to come, and Bowman wanted them to get more ice time. That meant Yzerman was on the trading block. At least publicly, Yzerman had resigned himself to the fact that he might be traded. "It's up to management. I don't really have much to say," said Yzerman after a practice in the dressing room. "I feel comfortable with the whole situation and I'm not taking it personally right now."

No moves had been made by the October 13 home opener. As usual, it was a packed house at Joe Louis Arena. The banners for the Red Wings' Presidents' Trophy, Western Conference titles and Central Division titles from the previous seasons were unfurled in the rafters. Each Detroit player was also introduced as he skated out and stood on one of the blue lines. When Detroit public address announcer Budd Lynch said, "No. 19, Steve Yzerman," the crowd drowned out the last name with a tremendous ovation. It continued as the fans all stood up and started chanting, "Stevie! Stevie! Stevie!" This continued for well over a minute. Red Wings fans had spoken with their huge ovation for Yzerman. They wanted the captain to stay. After the game, Yzerman said he had been moved by the outpouring of affection. "I certainly appreciated that. I think every player would," he said. "...You get a rush. It just makes you feel good."

Yzerman also reached a career milestone during the 1995-96 season when he scored the 500th goal of his NHL career in a 4-2 victory over Colorado. For the second time during the season, the JLA crowd gave Yzerman a deafening ovation and filled the building with chants of "Stevie! Stevie! Stevie!" As his teammates mobbed and congratulated Yzerman after the goal had been scored, one of the most special congratulations came from Ciccarelli, who had scored the 500th goal of his career during the 1993-94 season. "Yeah, I was happy for him. I went through the same thing. I'm happy to see him get it at home," said Ciccarelli after the game. "...I told him I've got a lot of stuff for him to sign." Ciccarelli added that the moment was made even sweeter by the fact that Yzerman had persevered through all of the trade rumors of the past. He added: "I knew he was happy. I saw him on the ice, coming to the bench, and he had the biggest smile on his face."

> "Having to score a goal to set a record is a lot tougher than getting an assist. He [Yzerman] scored on his chance, and **he did it at home. That's perfect.** There's only 22 guys who have done what he's done, and that makes it special."
>
> PAUL COFFEY, CAROLINA HURRICANES DEFENSEMAN

Yzerman said he was taken aback by the whole scene after he had deposited the puck behind Patrick Roy for number 500. "The players and everybody coming onto the ice, we were just kind of hanging around a bit," said Yzerman after the game. "They were just kind of laughing and rubbing their gloves in my face. That was the most fun. I'm just really pleased that everyone came out there [on the ice]. That was the most fun part of it. I guess the thing that caught me off guard was the fact that everybody was out there before I knew it." Despite his usual aversion to attention from the media, Yzerman said that he didn't feel any extra pressure after he had gotten close to goal number 500. "I wasn't relieved, because I've enjoyed all of the attention and everything that went with it," he said.

chapter four: A New Era

This signaled a significant change in his attitude about his hockey career. Maybe it was his near trade to Ottawa or maybe it was the fact that the Red Wings had gotten to the Stanley Cup finals the year before. Or maybe it was the fact that he had proven that he could continue to be an offensive force under the Wings' new team-oriented system. Or maybe it was a combination of all three. But Yzerman began to enjoy life as an NHL player more. "I remember him saying something like, 'I'm going to enjoy things more. I'm going to do more things with the guys,'" said Darren Pang.

As the regular season, which had been dominated by the Red Wings, wound down to a close, the focus was on the Wings' chances to win the Stanley Cup. They were the prohibitive favorites and had all of the pressure on them. The Wings eliminated the Winnipeg Jets in the first round. Detroit's second-round opponents were the St. Louis Blues, and the series would go to a deciding Game 7 in Detroit.

Game 7 was scoreless through regulation time and after the first overtime period. Just over a minute into the second overtime period, Yzerman stole the puck from Wayne Gretzky outside the Red Wings blue line and skated towards the St. Louis zone on the right wing. Just as Yzerman skated over the blue line, he cocked his stick and let go a high slap shot which sizzled over goalie Jon Casey's stick side and into the top of the net. Thanks to Yzerman, the Red Wings won the series and advanced to the Western Conference finals.

RED WINGS RECORD | single-season most points: 155 (1988-89)

When the puck went into the net, Yzerman leaped into the air in celebration and was mobbed by his teammates for the second time in the 1995-96 season. "I was just trying to get it past the defenseman's leg," said Yzerman after the game. "I looked up and saw that it had went over his blocker, and I was just as stunned as anybody."

It was the general consensus that it was fitting for Yzerman to score a double-overtime game and series winner for the Red Wings. "It's great to see Stevie get it," said defenseman Mike Ramsey. "He had all kinds of criticism and he had to put up with all of the trade talks. So it was kind of sweet," added Red Wings owner Mike Ilitch.

The Red Wings' opponents in the Western Conference finals were the Colorado Avalanche, who would send the Wings packing in six games. Though he was disappointed that he and his teammates had been denied hockey's Holy Grail, despite having one of the greatest regular seasons in NHL history, Yzerman was once again complimented by Ilitch on the way he had played throughout the season and in the playoffs. "Steve played with so much heart and played defensive hockey for the good of the team," he said. "Steve Yzerman is the ultimate, total player. I think he exemplifies heart."

Yzerman had led Detroit in playoff scoring with eight goals and 12 assists. As the Red Wings cleaned out their lockers and got ready to head home for the summer, Yzerman said that he wanted to be a Red Wing for life. "I'm here as long as they want me," he said.

Hockey Tips for Young Players: WINNING FACE-OFFS

Concentrating and knowing the player whom you are going against are the keys. You may need to anticipate when the referee is going to drop the puck instead of waiting until the puck is actually released. Is the opposing player stronger or quicker than you are? If you're quicker, you may be able to beat him cleanly. Or if he's quicker but you're stronger, you may be able to outmuscle him for the puck, even though he makes the first contact. You may also have to tie him up off the face-off and kick the puck to a teammate. One thing is for sure: No matter how good you are at taking face-offs, you will lose your share of them. And when you do, you have to remember to stay with the opposing center after he's beaten you on the draw. This is particularly important on face-offs in your defensive zone.

YZERMAN'S OFF-SEASON ENDED EARLIER THAN USUAL. HE WAS SELECTED TO PLAY FOR TEAM CANADA IN THE WORLD CUP OF HOCKEY TO BE HELD IN BOTH EUROPE AND NORTH AMERICA. ALTHOUGH TEAM USA WON THE TOURNAMENT BY DEFEATING TEAM CANADA IN THE FINALS, YZERMAN GOT A CHANCE TO OBSERVE A BIG, TOUGH AND TALENTED WINGER WHO WAS A SNIPER AND COULD PLAY IN ALL SITUATIONS. BRENDAN SHANAHAN WAS JUST WHAT THE RED WINGS NEEDED.

NHL | fifty goal seasons: 5

chapter five: Finally...The Cup

After teaming with Shanahan in the World Cup of Hockey, Yzerman told Red Wings management that they should look into obtaining him. The trade was finally completed on October 9, 1996. Shanahan arrived in the Red Wings locker room just as the team was about to take the ice for warm-ups. Yzerman told his teammates to wait until Shanahan got dressed so that he could take the ice with his new team. Not only did the Red Wings have another topnotch player, but they had one who was talented, big and tough. Shanahan was the symbol of the way the Red Wings needed to change their team in order to win the Stanley Cup.

" Sometimes, because of his offensive numbers, people just think of him as an offensive player. But I really haven't played with a better defensive forward."

BRENDAN SHANAHAN,
RED WINGS TEAMMATE

Hockey Tips for Young Players:
BACKCHECKING

As a forward trailing the play into your own zone when the other team has possession, don't think you don't have any defensive responsibilities. Look around. If there is an opposing player within 10-15 feet of you, he's now your man. Stick with him. Oftentimes, it's not the first wave of a rush that scores a goal but a "late" man who either scores on a rebound or off a drop or centering pass.

In November, Yzerman signed a four-year deal with the Red Wings that included provisions for him to work in the Red Wings organization when his playing career ended. After he signed the deal, he talked about how happy he was to know that he would remain in Detroit. "Detroit has become my home. My daughter was born here," he said. "This is where we call home. When the season is over and we go on vacation, when we talk about going home, we're talking about going here."

On February 19, 1997, Yzerman passed another career milestone when he played his 1000th NHL game in a 4-0 victory over the Calgary Flames. "It's pretty special," Yzerman said after the game. "I've played with a lot of guys and have been through a lot. A lot of different teams, but one uniform."

As the season progressed, the Red Wings weren't the dominant team they had been in previous regular seasons. In fact they were inconsistent. It was almost as if they had figured out that it wasn't necessary to dominate during the regular season. All that was necessary was to get a decent playoff position and then turn it up in the playoffs. With their talent, it was almost a cinch that they would finish in the top four.

The Red Wings coasted into the playoffs with the third-best record in the Western Conference. Unlike previous seasons, there was no pressure of having been the conference's top team during the regular season. The Red Wings weren't the team that every other team in the conference was "gunning" for, and they were happy not to have that burden. "The last couple of years, we've had the pressure on us as favorites," Nicklas Lidstrom said. "It's a lot easier to go into the playoffs without that pressure on you."

NHL | career playoff games played: 145

chapter five: Finally...The Cup

The Red Wings swept through St. Louis, Anaheim and Colorado on their way to a match-up with the Philadelphia Flyers in the Stanley Cup finals. The Red Wings quickly achieved a 2-0 lead in the series and were halfway to the team's first Stanley Cup in 42 years when the series moved to Detroit. They hammered the Flyers in Game 3 with a 6-1 victory.

Between Games 3 and 4, Pang talked about how he looked forward to seeing Yzerman's playful smile as he finally lifted the Stanley Cup. "He doesn't play for the Porsche, he doesn't play for the big house. He plays because he wants to be a winner," said Pang. "He's never been a winner before. It'll be fun looking at him. It'll be fun seeing that smile. You saw it when he held the Clarence Campbell Trophy two years ago, you saw it last year when he scored his 500th goal and his daughter sees it a lot. That's it."

Everyone expected the Flyers to just roll over in Game 4, but it would be their best game of the series. They took the play to the Red Wings for much of the first period, but goaltender Mike Vernon was up to the task. The Red Wings were up 2-1 with less than 15 seconds remaining in the game when Canadian Broadcasting Company play-by-play man Bob Cole summed up the feelings that many hockey fans have about Yzerman. As the teams lined up for the game's final face-off at center ice, he said on CBC's telecast of the game, "Steve Yzerman. On the ice, as he should be. At center, where he belongs."

And as the final seconds ticked down to zero, the puck came into the Red Wings zone. Vernon was behind the net in order to play the puck as it caromed around the boards, when the buzzer sounded to end the game and declare the Red Wings the 1997 Stanley Cup champions. Yzerman was the first player to his goaltender. They jumped into each other's arms, quickly followed by their teammates.

46 | NHL | career playoff goals scored: 61 | sixty-one

As is the tradition, Commissioner Gary Bettman was ushered onto the ice to present the Conn Smythe Trophy and the Stanley Cup. Vernon was presented with the Conn Smythe Trophy. Then the crowd started chanting, "Stevie! Stevie! Stevie!" in anticipation of Bettman presenting the Cup to Yzerman. As he accepted the Cup, Yzerman flashed the smile that Pang and Red Wings fans had been waiting so long to see. At that moment, ESPN analyst Bill Clement –

a former NHL player – said: "Nobody deserves the Stanley Cup more than that man right there." After Yzerman took his turn around the ice with the Cup, he went over to where Ilitch was seated and handed it to the team's owner, who held it aloft before handing it back to Yzerman.

After the game, while still on the ice, Yzerman talked about finally winning hockey's most prized trophy. "This is unbelievable. It's been a long time for Detroit. It's been a long time for me in Detroit. It's just been a wild year," he said. "It was the most rewarding and greatest moment of my career. As my career went on, the one thing I lacked in Detroit was a championship. I wanted desperately to have my name on the Stanley Cup with all the great players on it. Maybe 20 or 30 years from now I can go look at the trophy and see my name on it."

chapter five: Finally...The Cup

Both Yzerman and the Red Wings had attained hockey's Holy Grail. But the Red Wings players talked about how happy they were for their captain. "This guy deserves the Cup like nobody," said Konstantinov. "Everybody's been playing for this guy. We wanted to win the Cup for him." Said Shanahan: "As much as we wanted to win the Cup for ourselves, we all wanted to win it for Stevie. Me and Darren [McCarty] were telling players to hold back and let Stevie take the first lap with the Cup by himself. We got more joy out of seeing him hoist the Cup than we did holding it ourselves." Former Red Wings great and Hall of Famer Ted Lindsay saluted Yzerman's contribution. "I'm very happy for Steve," said Lindsay. "He came here when the Red Wings had absolutely nothing, and he owes the Red Wings absolutely nothing. Nothing makes me happier than seeing him carry the Cup."

> "Everybody wanted to win it [the Stanley Cup] for himself No. 1 and for him [Yzerman] No. 2."
>
> JOE KOCUR, RED WINGS TEAMMATE

After their celebration on the ice and in their Joe Louis Arena dressing room, the Red Wings proceeded to a suburban Detroit restaurant for a victory celebration. When that celebration broke up in the wee hours of the morning, the Cup was placed in Yzerman's car, and he and his wife, Lisa, took it home. Upon arrival, Yzerman placed it in the middle of the family's kitchen. It's unlikely that he's ever enjoyed a breakfast more than the one he had the following day.

Everybody was happy. For six days, all was right for the Red Wings and the city of Detroit. But the seventh day would bring tragedy. On June 13, 1997, a limousine carrying Red Wings defensemen Vladimir Konstantinov and Viacheslav Fetisov and team masseur Sergei Mnatsakanov was involved in a serious accident. The ramifications of that crash would spread throughout the Red Wings organization, the Detroit area and across the entire National Hockey League. Not only did the accident end the careers of both Konstantinov and Mnatsakanov, but it forever changed their lives and the lives of those who love them. Both remained in wheelchairs as of the summer of 1999.

When the Red Wings players and officials got calls with the terrible news, they all immediately headed to the hospital. Under any circumstances, this would have been a tragedy. But it was even more so for the Red Wings because they had become such a close-knit group. The players and other members of the organization were at the hospital all night. The following day, a shaken Yzerman addressed the assembled media with his somber teammates standing behind him. "As you can see, several of the players and members of the organization have been here all night," he said. "We ask for your support, we're all devastated." Yzerman also made a request. He said the Red Wings were like a family and that family was going through a terrible tragedy. He then asked the reporters to put themselves in the situation and not call players to get quotes about the tragedy for a respectful period of time.

NHL | career playoff assists: 87

chapter five: Finally...The Cup

But when the 1997-98 season began, despite the tragic loss of their best defenseman, it was as if the Red Wings hadn't missed a beat. Yzerman regained his spot as the team's leading scorer but only had 24 goals and 45 assists for 69 points. However, on October 29, 1997, he put his name alongside one of hockey's immortals. That night, in a 4-3 victory over the San Jose Sharks, Yzerman scored the 544th goal of his career to tie him with Maurice "Rocket" Richard for 15th place on the all-time list.

After the game, reporters asked Yzerman how it felt to tie Richard for the record. "I don't compare myself to a player of that stature and accomplishment," said Yzerman. "In my opinion, I never saw him play, but Maurice Richard was probably one of the greatest players of all time. And I don't put myself among those players. It's nice to see your name among those players."

Yzerman got more great news late in November. For the first time in history, NHL players would participate in the 1998 Winter Olympics. The league would be shut down for 17 days in February, while the best NHL players competed for their countries. Not only was Yzerman a Team Canada pick, he was also named an alternate captain. "It's a real honor to be an assistant captain. I'm really quite surprised," he said. "Everybody has pride in their country, and I'm sure some guys have their reasons for not going. It's an opportunity to play on a dream team with the best players in the world."

In February, the Olympics would prove to be pivotal for Yzerman. The Yzerman who returned to the Red Wings after the Olympics wasn't the same one who had left for Japan. As far as quickness and explosiveness were concerned, this was the Yzerman from about eight years before. He was beating players with his speed and making great plays with his patented rush into the opposing team's zone, once again overpowering goalies with wicked slap shots and wrist shots.

He had 11 goals and 15 assists for 26 points in his first 19 games after the Olympics. And he remained just as good defensively. "The biggest thing that energized me this year was the Olympics. Six games of that pace and skating on the big surface really helped," said Yzerman. "When I got back, I was taking the puck and skating instead of getting the puck and looking around."

The Red Wings finished second in the Western Conference, six points behind the Dallas Stars. In the postseason, the Red Wings would defeat Phoenix, St. Louis and Dallas on their way to a second-consecutive Stanley Cup final. The Red Wings opponents were the underdog Washington Capitals. As they had the previous season, the Red Wings took a 3-0 series lead. Game 4 was almost anticlimactic. With the score 4-1 in Detroit's favor and the game's final few minutes ticking down, defenseman Vladimir Konstantinov's presence was acknowledged. The Red Wings banged their sticks on the boards and the ice and whooped it up for their injured teammate.

NHL | career playoff points: 148

148

chapter five: Finally...The Cup

After the Red Wings had won their second-consecutive Stanley Cup and were celebrating, Konstantinov was wheeled onto the ice. And in one of the most stirring and emotional victory celebrations in recent memory, Yzerman took the Cup, skated over to Konstantinov and placed it in his lap. Yzerman, Shanahan, Darren McCarty, Fetisov and Igor Larionov all helped push Konstantinov around the ice as their jubilant teammates followed. Asked if he thought Konstantinov realized what was happening, McCarty said, "You bet he knows, baby!"

The previous season, there had been no clear consensus about who had been the Red Wings' best playoff performer. But this season there was no doubt about it: Yzerman was the clear choice. Yzerman's 24 points tied a Detroit team record, which had been set in the 1995 playoffs. And Yzerman won the Conn Smythe Trophy as the playoff MVP. In his 15th season, he had finally won his first major individual award. But, more importantly, he had won his second-straight Stanley Cup.

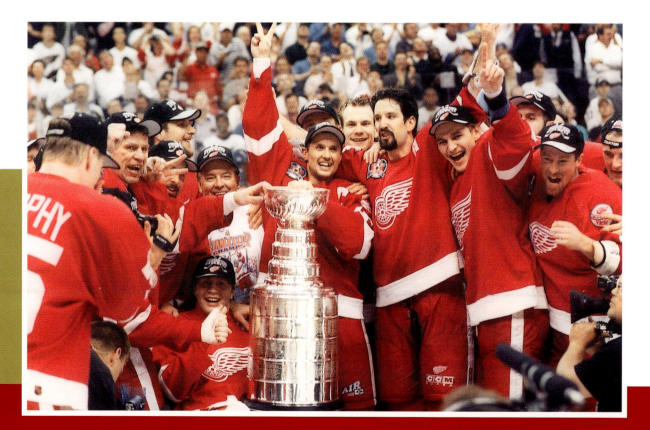

While the Red Wings would fall short of their third-straight Stanley Cup, 1998-99 would be a banner season for Yzerman. He was the team's best and most consistent player as he led Detroit in scoring with 29 goals and 45 assists for 74 points. He continued to be the explosive offensive threat that he had been following the Olympics the previous season.

Detroit finished the season with an 8-1-2 flurry and won their first six playoff games. They eliminated the Anaheim Mighty Ducks in a four-game sweep in the first round and won the first two games of the second round against the Colorado Avalanche. Yzerman had eight goals in those six games and would finish the playoffs with nine. But the momentum suddenly shifted, and the Avalanche won the next four games to eliminate the Red Wings.

There would be no third-straight Stanley Cup, but Yzerman and the Red Wings had still come a long way. Yzerman had gone from being a shy but talented 18-year-old rookie on a losing team to a two-time Stanley Cup-winning captain of the NHL's most prominent franchise, whose numbers rank him among the all-time greats of hockey. "The ultimate hockey player," said Greg Stefan of Yzerman. "From his leadership and determination to his skill level to his work ethic. In Detroit now, he's everybody's hero if they're a hockey fan. He's been the captain for so many years. He's won the Stanley Cup. Now you can put Yzerman with guys like Howe, Lindsay and Abel."

Bowman

Since becoming the Red Wings coach in the 1993-94 season, Scotty Bowman has used Yzerman in every situation. Yzerman has responded by becoming one of the NHL's best two-way forwards. Not only has Yzerman skated a regular shift with numerous linemates, but he's also been a regular on the power play and penalty killing units. In addition to playing center, Yzerman has played both wing positions. Many times he has played all three forward positions in the same game. Bowman talks about Yzerman's talents and the veteran center's role with the team.

Steve Yzerman isn't just supremely talented, he also works extremely hard on the ice. When his teammates see how hard such a talented player works, they have no choice but to work hard themselves.

"It's more than just how he plays. It's how he reflects his play to the other players on the team. A lot of the time a star player has a lot of talent, and it will seem to the other players on the team that things come easy for him. But with Steve being a real hard worker in games and practices, he's a real good example for the other players, especially younger players."

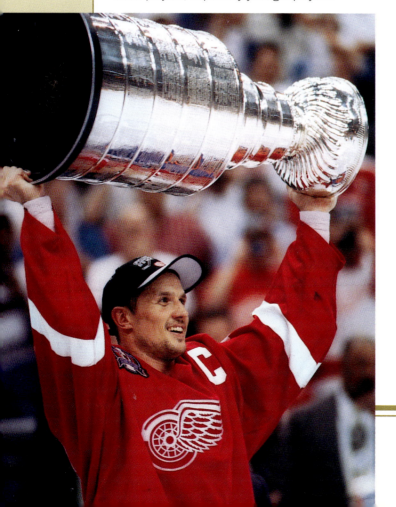

Yzerman doesn't just work on the offensive end, but he works just as hard defensively and on face-offs.

"I think as the team got stronger over the last five to six years, it definitely showed that he could play a complete game. It's tough when you don't have a lot of good players around you. He became a more complete player with the way he was used with his teammates. He does the kind of things that don't always show up in the stats."

Yzerman is one of the best conditioned athletes you'll find anywhere.

"He's an elite athlete. He's a big man, but he actually isn't a big person. But he does work on the physical part of his game. He keeps a close tab on his physical conditioning."

What's the strongest part of Yzerman's game on the ice?

"Probably stickhandling, which includes the fact that he doesn't throw the puck away. Stickhandling also means beating players one-on-one."

Yzerman has scored some seemingly impossible goals in his career by finding an angle that doesn't seem to be there.

"He can do a lot with his shot. He can put the puck where he wants to. He doesn't just shoot the puck at the net. He can pick openings."

Yzerman has a combination of determination and talent to respond with points when he feels he has been challenged.

"That's something you have to respect. You have to respect what kind of player he is. Generally speaking, if he gets his chances, he capitalizes. He's always been a sharpshooter."

Yzerman is very similar to one of his heroes, Bryan Trottier, as a player.

"They both were centers, obviously very strong two-way players. Not just point machines. They had very similar styles. Trottier played a lot of hockey with [Hall of Fame right wing] Mike Bossy. Steve has had a lot of linemates. They played in a lot of situations and had a lot of stamina. Both are very competitive. They have a lot of the same demeanor off the ice. Always trying to help out."

Steve Yzerman has a great work ethic.

"He's one of the players in the league – and there are a few – who come to work every day. You kind of have to shoo him off the practice ice."

Though quiet and unassuming, Yzerman is an incredible competitor who wants to win at all costs.

"Just because someone isn't outwardly emotional, it doesn't mean they don't have this burning desire to win."

ABOUT SCOTTY BOWMAN

IN A COACHING CAREER THAT HAS SPANNED FOUR DECADES, SCOTTY BOWMAN HOLDS JUST ABOUT EVERY SIGNIFICANT COACHING RECORD IN NHL HISTORY.

THAT INCLUDES THE NHL CAREER RECORDS FOR THE MOST VICTORIES AND GAMES COACHED. BOWMAN'S EIGHT STANLEY CUPS TIE HIM WITH MONTREAL LEGEND TOE BLAKE FOR THE ALL-TIME RECORD. AND HE'S THE ONLY COACH IN NHL HISTORY TO WIN THE STANLEY CUP WITH THREE DIFFERENT TEAMS.

BOWMAN BEGAN HIS COACHING CAREER WITH THE ST. LOUIS BLUES EARLY IN THE 1967-68 SEASON AND STAYED WITH THE BLUES UNTIL THE 1970-71 SEASON, WHEN HE COACHED THE TEAM FOR 26 GAMES. AFTER THAT, HE WENT TO THE MONTREAL CANADIENS FOR THE 1971-72 SEASON. HE LED THE CANADIENS TO FIVE STANLEY CUPS IN EIGHT SEASONS. HE THEN MOVED ON TO THE BUFFALO SABRES, WHERE HE SHARED THE GENERAL MANAGER AND COACHING DUTIES FROM 1979-80 UNTIL 1986-87.

AFTER A STINT AS A CBC HOCKEY ANALYST FOR THREE SEASONS, HE JOINED THE PITTSBURGH PENGUINS AS THEIR PLAYER PERSONNEL MANAGER IN JUNE 1990. HE FULFILLED THAT ROLE FOR TWO SEASONS BEFORE STEPPING BEHIND THE PENGUINS BENCH AS COACH IN 1991-92. THAT SEASON, BOWMAN COACHED THE PENGUINS TO THEIR SECOND-STRAIGHT STANLEY CUP.

HE WAS EVENTUALLY HIRED AS THE RED WINGS COACH FOR THE 1993-94 SEASON. IN ADDITION TO LEADING DETROIT TO THE 1997 AND 1998 STANLEY CUPS, BOWMAN COACHED THE 1995-96 TEAM TO AN ALL-TIME NHL RECORD 62 WINS.

BORN SEPTEMBER 18, 1933, BOWMAN AND HIS WIFE, SUELLA, HAVE FIVE CHILDREN: ALICIA, DAVID, STANLEY, BOB AND NANCY.

GAME-DAY routine

WHEN THE RED WINGS PLAY AT HOME, HERE IS WHAT STEVE YZERMAN'S DAY WILL LOOK LIKE:

8:30 a.m.	Wake up.
9 a.m.	Head down to Joe Louis Arena for the morning skate.
9:30 a.m.	Arrive at Joe Louis Arena.
9:50 a.m.	Get massage and do a crossword puzzle.
10:30 a.m.	Take the ice for the morning skate.
11:15 a.m.	Most of the NHL's star players leave the ice as early as 15 to 20 minutes into the game-day skate. Yzerman, however, loves to practice and is on the ice as much as possible. He's always one of the last players to exit the ice.
12 p.m.	Head back home.
2 p.m.	Take a nap.
4:45 p.m.	Head to Joe Louis Arena for the game.
5:15 p.m.	Arrive at Joe Louis Arena.
5:45 p.m.	Tape sticks.
6:15 p.m.	Do stretches and pliometrics (squats, lunges, etc.).
6:30 p.m.	Get dressed.
6:45 p.m.	As captain, Yzerman gives the word to the rest of his teammates when to take the ice.
7:30 p.m.	Game begins.
10:30 p.m.	The Red Wings hit their exercise bikes for a cool down. As one of the most fit and hardest working workout warriors in the NHL, Yzerman usually takes longer to complete his postgame workout than most. The players then get any needed medical treatments, shower and get dressed. After answering questions from the media, they meet their wives and girlfriends and split up into groups to go have dinner.